Bouquets

a year of flowers for the bride

Marsha Heckman

Photographs by Richard Jung

stewart, tabori & chang

NEW YORK

Published by
Stewart, Tabori & Chang
115 West 18th Street
New York, NY 10011

Canadian Distribution:
Canadian Manda Group
One Atlantic Avenue, Suite 105
Toronto, Ontario M6K 3E7 Canada

Library of Congress Cataloging-in-Publication Data
Heckman, Marsha.
    Bouquets: a year of flowers for the bride/Marsha Heckman;
photography by Richard Jung.
    p.   cm.
    ISBN 1-55670-966-8
    1. Bridal bouquets.   I. Title.
    SB449.5.B7H43   2000   99-31611
    745.92'6—dc21   CIP

Printed in China

10 9 8 7 6

Stewart, Tabori & Chang is a subsidiary of

LA MARTINIÈRE GROUPE

CREDITS

Wedding Attire

Cover and page 80: "Platinum Ice" gown by Angel Sanchez, courtesy of Marina Morrison Ltd. Bridal Salon, San Francisco, Calif. (415) 984-9360; pages 14 and 41: Bridal gowns by RICARDO; page 18: Bridal gown by Jade Daniels; page 22: Coat dress by Helen Morley; page 26: Custom wedding dress by Sylvia Bentcheva Couture, Larkspur, Calif.; page 32: "Tulle Cloud" gown by Ulla Maija; page 54: Daisy sheath by Richard Glasgow; page 60: Beaded gown by Badgley Mischka; pages 72 and 93: Bridal gowns by Richard Glasgow; page 77: Bridal gown by Angel Sanchez; page 94: Dress by Beverly Siri

Accessories and Props

Page 12: Silver tussie mussie holder courtesy of Linen & Lace, Washington, Mo. (800) 332-LACE; pages 31, 32, 34, 38, 41, and 42: Ribbons courtesy of BRITEX Fabrics, San Francisco, Calif. (415) 392-3906; pages 32 and 34: Garden roses courtesy of Garden Valley Ranch, Petaluma, Calif. (707) 792-0377; page 51: Antique lines courtesy of Pauline G. Robert, Belvedere, Calif.; page 60: Seashell and bead flowers courtesy of Claudia Allin and Cathy Obiedo; pages 70, 78, and 95: Linens courtesy of Emi Hale Home Collection, Corte Madera, Calif.; page 81: Rhinestone trim courtesy of BRITEX Fabrics, San Francisco, Calif. (415) 392-3906; page 90: Swarovski crystal snowflakes from the collection of John Bani, The Burlwood Gallery, Sausalito, Calif.; page 98: Live violet heart courtesy of Ano Nuevo Flower Growers, Pescadero, Calif. (650) 879-0389

contents

Dedication

Dedicated to the women of flowers in my family:
My mother Diane, Tante and Grandma,
And my sisters, Claudia and Cathy.

Introduction

Years ago my friend Susy Pollard, who owned *The Secret Garden* flower shop in Sausalito, California, asked me to help her with a wedding. At four o'clock in the morning she took me to the San Francisco Flower Mart. Imagine huge warehouses filled with thousands and thousands of flowers. The smell was intoxicating in the morning air. I was stunned to see vendors surrounded by endless buckets of lilacs, peonies, daffodils, callas, freesia, and tulips. There must have been a million roses. One vendor had nothing but violets in giant hoop handle baskets; another sold bundles of blossoming tree branches six feet high. I was in heaven. I wanted to live there.

In my family everyone loves flowers. My mother and grandmother shared a passion for roses. Tante had a cool, green garden with flowers to cut in every season. We were taught to notice and appreciate flowers, to delight in their breathtaking beauty and perfection. We were encouraged to breathe in the delicious scents that overwhelmed our noses with pleasure and tickled the memory. We became aware of the amazing varieties of shapes and colors that dazzle the eye—from a tiny bell-shaped lily of the valley to huge, vibrant sunflowers and dahlias.

I remember making bouquets of miniature pink roses for all the bridesmaids in a doll wedding. The bride doll carried a single white lilac with streamers of bias tape from my mother's sewing box. The first real bridal bouquets I made were for the weddings of my sisters. Cathy carried a little daisy nosegay with turquoise and white dangling ribbons tied into little lover's knots. I made Claudia a bouquet of white roses, mistletoe, and tiny silver bells for her Christmas wedding. I made bridal bouquets for all my friends, corsages for my sons' prom dates, and flower garlands for my daughter's horse in the Mill Valley Day parade. I arranged bouquets for graduations and showers, and for every holiday and dinner party.

Susy taught me the professional way to prepare flowers, to wire and tape them. After the flowers for the bride's bouquet were groomed, she told me to make a bridesmaid's bouquet. "Start with a 'star' flower, then keep putting flowers into your hand one at a time," she said, "until they speak to you." And the flowers did speak to me. They told me that they wanted to bend a particular way and show their faces at an angle that pleased them. They cuddled right up to some flowers and fought others with clashing color or rigid stem. Then there was a bouquet in my hand. Flowers are like stained glass; when you use such a beautiful medium it's not very hard to make art. Since then I've designed the flowers for a hundred weddings from my workshop at home.

I created *Bouquets* to give brides a book that would inspire them to make their wedding bouquets beautiful, personal, and meaningful. It is a guide for the bride-to-be and generous volunteer, sister or friend, to make the wedding bouquets at home. Loved ones are happy to make a special contribution to a wedding, and their involvement is a gift. Or you may use this book to show your favorite florist exactly what kind of bouquet you want. *Bouquets* is organized to show you flowers available in every month at the local flower shop or in the garden. There is a "recipe" for each bouquet. Many are easy, some are more challenging. Begin by reading the "Making the Bouquets" chapter, which explains the processes for grooming the flowers and gives you specific instructions for wiring and taping, using ribbon, and making pretty handles. I strongly encourage you to make a practice bouquet in advance to determine how long it will take. And it will make a lovely centerpiece for the bridal shower.

It is a sensual experience to carry flowers. When you walk down the aisle on your wedding day you hold memories in your hands, and beauty and perfume. You carry flowers that you will remember all your life. A bouquet is a token of honor. Heroes and visiting royalty are always presented with bouquets. We give bouquets to beauty queens and contest winners. And every bride carries one.

Your first decision is whether your bridal bouquet will be white, colored, or both. Do you want a bouquet of one kind of flower, or several? My favorite is one variety, or two flowers in the same color palette. White flowers with white ribbon is the purest and most traditional bride's bouquet. Many white flowers have tinges of pink, green, cream, yellow, peach, or lavender. Mixing white with color makes a more dimensional-looking bouquet.

Choose your favorites from flowers you can reasonably expect to find on your wedding day. Each flower has a somewhat predictable growing season. Amaryllis, violets, dahlias, daffodils, forget-me-nots, peonies, lilacs, and camellias are only available for a short time. Your nurseryman or florist can give you information about blooming times in your area.

Many flowers are available out of season in the flower shop. Hothouse roses and chrysanthemums are provided all year. Orchids and stephanotis grow year round in the tropics for export, as well as tulips and lily of the valley from Holland and France. Hydrangea, gardenia, freesia, and delphinium are available from commercial growers for several months. But it is really best to rely on flowers in their season, and it will save you money. You are not limited to cut flowers. Blooms from shrubs and potted plants can make a beautiful bouquet. Friends and family who are gardeners are a valuable resource for advice and for flowers. With enough notice they may grow your bouquet for you.

Will your flowers be a replication of a bouquet in an old photograph or in a picture from a current bridal mag-

azine? Are you looking for something fresh and different or very traditional? Romantic or architectural? Will your wedding be a very formal affair or will it be casual? Will the ceremony take place in a garden or in a cathedral? A loose bouquet of lots of different flowers in an organic shape is a free and casual look. A structured arrangement of one or two varieties of flowers with pearl sprays and silk ribbons is elegant and formal.

The shape of the bouquet should complement your dress. A bridal gown with a slim skirt looks best with a loose, natural-shaped bouquet of several flowers—like pincushion, love-in-a-mist, and daisies (page 54). A wide satin skirt adorned with lace or beading needs a circle of roses (page 85) or a dahlia dome (page 64). An oval bouquet of sweet peas (page 46) or orchids with an opulent bow on the handle (page 78) will not hide seed pearls and embroidery on your dress. A long cascade of wheat and waxflower (page 77) or chrysanthemums and asters dripping with ribbons (page 71) is perfect for a floor-length taffeta ball gown, while a side-arm tulip bouquet (page 14) is beautiful on a ballerina skirt made of layers of tulle. A tight stephanotis nosegay with a jewel-accented handle (page 80) will complement a soft chiffon dress or a designer evening gown. Whether it is unstructured or tight, round, oval, or heart-shaped, make sure your bouquet is large enough for the look you want, but not so big it will overwhelm your dress.

The tradition and history of flowers deepens the meaning of a bouquet. Hold heather in your arms to remember a Scottish ancestor, or recall the passion of a favorite love story (page 93). Carry a Victorian nosegay of violets (page 99), a cascade of wheat like a bride in ancient Rome (page 77), or an Elizabethan bouquet of herbs (page 50).

Some brides prefer to carry a single flower—a rose, an orchid, or one huge peony embellished with ribbon (page 25). A bride-to-be may choose to hold a fan (page 68) or her mother's prayer book decorated with hyacinth florets (page 17). A tiny violet posy wrapped in an heirloom handkerchief (page 100) or a little bunch of lily of the valley in an antique silver holder are wonderful accessories. A treasured cameo or rosary, a lock of your beloved's hair, a seashell found on the beach where you met, or his first love letter to you can be tucked among the flowers.

Attendants' bouquets should complement the bridal flowers, and they usually provide color. A bridesmaid's dress and flowers in the same color has a soft look, but contrast makes the bouquet pop—hot pink anemones against a navy blue bridesmaid's gown (page 94), or golden yellow sunflowers (page 66) with a chocolate taffeta dress. Elaborate or simple, bridesmaid's bouquets can be identical or made in different shapes with the same flowers and ribbons. Embellish them with trinkets and lace. The groom's boutonniere (pages 36-37) is plucked from the bridal flowers, and his grooms-

men's flowers should match the bridesmaids' flowers. Flower girls add sweetness and charm to your wedding party. Make them matching bouquets that fit tiny hands, or give them flower-covered hoops (page 23), or baskets brimming with petals (page 34) or lavender.

When I began to write *Bouquets,* I wanted to know why brides carry flowers. I learned that the custom began, as so many traditions do, with pure superstition. Certain herbs were believed to be a magical protection against the jealous evil spirits who would be roused by the marriage celebration. To ward off these demons, the groom wore herbs in his clothing, the bride carried them in her hands.

I discovered the charming language of flowers from the Victorian Age and how secret messages were communi-cated in a bouquet. Lovers shared a clandestine code—each word represented by a flower—and gave each other little bouquets called tussie mussies (page 12). The Victorian language of flowers may inform your choices in another memorable or romantic way. The bride's bouquet can represent the qualities of the couple and their hopes for the future: Roses for true love, sweet peas for pleasure, ivy mean-ing fidelity, wheat to bring abundance, and stephanotis promising wedded bliss.

Bouquets was written to encourage the bride to look for meaning in her wedding flowers, and to consider making her own bouquet at home. Personalizing your bou-quet with thoughtful choices of flowers is an opportunity for you to express your own style. A wedding bouquet is more than beautiful flowers that look nice with the bridal gown. The perfect handful of flowers will honor tradition, communicate a message, and enrich your memories.

Marsha Heckman
Mill Valley, California
May 1999

This is a time for flowers.

May each of them give to you not only its beauty and fragrance,

but also the symbolic meaning that human experience has added to them.

—A Bridal Blessing by Welleran Poltarnees

March

Lady Mary Wortley Montague, wife of the British ambassador to Constantinople, introduced the Eastern concept of flower language to English society in the early eighteenth century. She assigned individual sentiments and meanings to each flower according to the custom in Turkey, where unmarried women were not permitted to speak to men. She published her journal, *Turkish Letters*, which was shared and copied by romantic Europeans.

Charlotte de la Tour's 1819 version, *Le Language de Fleurs*, enjoyed a wild popularity throughout the Victorian Age. Flowers became a means of clandestine correspondence between chaperoned lovers, a code used to communicate a secret message with a bouquet.

Tussie Mussie

IRIS: "I Have a Message"

WHITE ROSE: Girlhood Innocence

DAFFODIL: Sweet Disposition
Regard; Devotion

BLUE HYACINTH: Constancy

VIOLET: Faithfulness

IVY: Fidelity in Marriage; Wedded Love

The language of flowers is the code that reveals a message in this tussie mussie, a little bouquet in a silver holder. The iris means "I have a message," and the flowers tell the groom what his shy bride wants him to know:

"I bring to you my girlhood innocence and my sweet disposition. I promise my regard and devotion, my love and constant fidelity in our marriage."

4 miniature daffodils
4 miniature iris
10 miniature roses
12 stems grape hyacinth (muscari)
6 violets
1 stem needlepoint ivy
florist tape
1 facial tissue
Tussie Mussie holder

Make this bouquet the night before the wedding.
Arrange the flowers in your hand, adding one flower at a time. Add the ivy to the bottom of the bouquet; tape the stems together neatly and trim them.
Fold the tissue and wrap it around the stems. Wet the tissue and cover it with tape.
Push the bouquet firmly into the holder. The tape will keep the tussie mussie in place.
Put the bouquet in the refrigerator until shortly before the ceremony.

Perfect Love

TULIP: Declaration of Love; Perfect Love A thousand years ago, tulips, called *lále*, grew in profusion in Persia, Russia, and the Ottoman Empire. The Ambassador of the Holy Roman Empire to Sultan Suleiman, the Magnificent of Turkey brought back tulip bulbs for the gardens of Emperor Ferdinand I in Vienna. In Constantinople, men wore turbans, often with a *lále* tucked into a fold. Europeans confused the name of the flower with *tulipan*, the word for turban.

French tulips are the largest variety, with big flowers and long stems. Dutch tulips are the standard size. Small tulips are usually hothouse grown and readily available.

20 French tulips
20 Dutch tulips
10 small tulips with gracefully curved stems
$^1/_2$ yard 3-inch-wide ribbon
1 yard 2-inch-wide decorative ribbon
vinyl tape
corsage pins

Begin making this bouquet the day before the wedding.

To force the stems of the small tulips to curve, place the tulips in a container filled with water. Place a light below the tulips. Within an hour they will bow toward the light.

Groom all the tulips, removing the leaves and any bruised petals.

Lay out the French and Dutch tulips, longest stems first. With the tulips in evenly spaced rows, create a diamond pattern, adding flowers to make wider rows toward the center, then decreasing the number of flowers toward the bottom.

Tape the stems together every five or six stems, forming a handle at the bottom point of the diamond.

Use the small, curved-stem tulips to conceal the handle, taping each flower in place.

Trim the stems.

Keep the bouquet in water in the refrigerator. Shortly before the wedding, remove the bouquet from the water and trim the stems again. Thoroughly dry the taped handle.

Wrap the handle with the 3-inch-wide ribbon and secure it with a row of corsage pins.

To finish, tie the decorative ribbon to the top of the handle in a four-loop bow.

Prayer Book

WHITE HYACINTH: Unobtrusive Loveliness; Unchanging Youth   In Ancient Greece, wedding attendants wore crowns of hyacinth florets to honor Ceres, the goddess of agriculture. Hyacinths, which were brought to the Mediterranean from Turkey, were found growing in the Coliseum in Rome and in the gardens of the Medicis in Florence. When a Genoese merchant ship laden with hyacinth bulbs was sunk in a storm off the coast of Holland, crates filled with the bulbs washed ashore and were broken open by the waves. The hyacinths grew along the Dutch coast and flourished there.

A bride often chooses to carry a prayer book adorned with flowers, rather than a bouquet. Whether it is a bible, a Catholic missal, or a prayer book, it is considered especially lucky if the book belonged to the bride's mother.

10 stems white muscari (grape hyacinth)
2 white hyacinth
$^1/_2$ yard $^1/_4$-inch-wide ribbon
2 yards $1^1/_2$-inch-wide velvet ribbon
light green florist tape
small boutonniere pins

Make this little corsage the night before the wedding.
Tape three muscari together. Cut the stems to 4 inches.

Pick the little flowers from the hyacinth and tape them neatly to the stems of the muscari, alternating hyacinth and muscari flowers five times, taping as you work down the stem.
Tie tiny bows of the $^1/_4$-inch ribbon in two or threes places on the stems and at the bottom.
Refrigerate in a loose plastic bag.
Shortly before the wedding, pin the corsage securely to the center of the velvet ribbon.
Tape two muscari and one hyacinth floret together. Tie with a bow of the $^1/_4$-inch ribbon. Pin to the velvet ribbon about 3 inches from the bottom.
Put the back part of the ribbon through the center of the book to hold it in place.

Elegant Wendy

CALLA: Magnificent Beauty
Elegance
Ardor

My daughter Wendy was courted on horseback in the Waimea canyon on the garden isle of Kauai. In the light of a full moon, Ken took her to a hidden valley filled with hundreds of callas, her favorite flower. Wendy knew that she loved him when he jumped from his horse to fill her arms with the beautiful blooms. Three years later, family and friends hiked into the same secret valley to gather callas for Wendy and Ken's unforgettable Hawaiian wedding.

18 callas of various sizes
36 faux pearl sprays (page 107)
2 yards 2-inch-wide double-faced satin ribbon
vinyl tape
corsage pins

Callas will stay fresh, so this bouquet can be made the day before the wedding.
On a work surface lay out the callas by size.
Gently remove the long yellow spadix from the center of each calla. (The spadix is actually the flower of the calla; the petals are known as bracts.)
Push one or two pearl sprays into the center of each calla.
Start making the bouquet with the smallest calla. Add flowers around it, using larger and larger callas as you work to create a tight, round bouquet. Keep the flowers quite close together, radiating from the center as if each calla is a petal of a larger flower.
Tape the stems, then trim them to about 6 inches.
Wrap the stems with ribbon, and secure it with corsage pins.
To finish, use the remaining ribbon to tie a bow just under the callas.
Place the bouquet in an upright container and keep in a cool place.

Affection

DAFFODIL: Returning Affection
Chivalry
Joy

Roman soldiers brought the daffodil to Britain where it was named affodyle, meaning "early arrival." On the Isle of Man, the daffodil is called the "goose lily," and in modern England it's often known as "daffy-down-dilly" or "Lent lily," because it blooms before Easter.

20 daffodils
1 yard 1-inch-wide wired gingham ribbon
1 yard 1-inch-wide striped ribbon
light green florist tape
corsage pin

Make this bouquet early on the day of the wedding.
Pick up the daffodils and hold them loosely. Adjust the flower heads to form a ball-shaped bouquet.
Tape the stems together close to the flower heads.

Leave the stems long, but trim them evenly at the bottom.
Put the bouquet into a container of water.
Cut one of the ribbons into three 12-inch pieces.
Shortly before the wedding, remove the bouquet from the water and dry the stems thoroughly.
Tie the pieces of ribbon into bows at three places on the stems, leaving room for your hand between the bows.
Starting at the bottom, cover the handle with the other ribbon by winding it around the stems between the bows. Secure with a corsage pin.

April

Flower petals play an important part in Hindu wedding rituals. At the close of the ceremony, the groom's brother or another relative showers the couple with petals to keep away evil spirits. On some Polynesian islands the bride walks on a path strewn with fragrant frangipani blossoms. And on the island of Jamaica, the bride sprinkles rose petals on the train of her gown for her bridal portrait.

For hundreds of years, little girls have been given the task of spreading blooms and petals before the bride in the procession to the church and down the aisle. This symbolizes a happy path through married life, with flowers all the way.

Fragrant Circle

FREESIA: Innocence   The circle, like the wedding ring, symbolizes eternity and endless love. The ring serves as a promise and represents the everlasting bonds of marriage. The Anglo-Saxon word for pledge is wed, as in the vow, "With this ring I thee wed."

A flower girl may carry a hoop covered with flowers instead of a nosegay or a basket.

30 stems freesia
8 branches lemon leaves
1½ yards 3-inch-wide grosgrain ribbon
12-inch-diameter wire wreath frame
vinyl tape

Make this hoop the day before the wedding.
Remove all the lemon leaves from the branches. Select forty-five perfect leaves. Wash the leaves, dry them, and set aside.
Cut the freesia stems to 4 inches and remove any wilted or broken blossoms.
Lay a lemon leaf lengthwise on the wire frame. Wrap the leaf around the frame and tape the stem end to it.
Place a freesia stem on top of the leaf and tape its stem to the frame.
Place the next leaf so it covers the freesia stem and tape it in place.
Continue taping a leaf, then a freesia, in the same direction until you have covered 2 inches less than half of the frame.
Cover 4 inches of the frame with leaves only to form a handle.
Now reverse the direction of the leaves and repeat the steps above until the frame is covered with alternating freesia and leaves.
Mist the hoop and keep it in a cool place overnight.
To finish, tie a fat bow to the handle with the streamers hanging inside the circle of flowers.

Michelle

WHITE LILAC: Innocence; Humility

PEONY: Bashful

Peonies have been cultivated in Asia for more than a thousand years. In Japan they graced the Imperial Gardens and came to represent prosperity because only the rich could afford to grow them. During the Tang Dynasty, the Chinese called the peony "hundred ounces of gold," a reference to the price of one plant. Once there was a Chinese princess who was forbidden by her father to speak to her true love. She wrote to him, one word at a time, on the petals of a white peony and dropped them into a stream in the hope that he would find them.

A single peony in full bloom, with a paper doily collar and a ribbon-wrapped stem, is a darling bouquet all by itself.

5 double-flowered peonies
10 stems lilac
5 stems freesia
2 yards 1 1/2-inch-wide ribbon
vinyl tape
corsage pin

Make this bouquet the day before the wedding.

Groom all the flowers, removing the leaves and any bruised or brown petals or florets.

Place two lilacs and one peony in your hand. Add a peony and two more lilacs, then repeat. Continue adding the flowers this way until you have a free-form round bouquet with lilacs all around its edge.

Add a stem of freesia wherever there is a space between the peonies and lilacs, then tape the stems together.

Trim the stems to 5 inches and cut a 1-inch slit up the woody stems of the lilacs to allow them to absorb water.

Put the bouquet into a container of water, mist it, cover it loosely with a plastic bag, and store it in the refrigerator.

Shortly before the wedding, dry the stems thoroughly, then trim neatly.

Cover the handle with ribbon, and secure it with a corsage pin.

To finish, double the remaining ribbon, and tie it into a bow around the handle at the base of the bouquet.

First Love

LILAC: First Emotions of Love
PEONY: Shyness

Lilacs have been found in gardens in India and the Himalayas, in Hungary and the Balkans, and along the ancient trade routes between China and Persia. The flower gets its name from the Arabic word *laylac*, which means "blue." At the turn of the twentieth century, lilacs were so popular in Europe that one Parisian flower merchant employed eighty people to handle his orders. Today, lilacs are grown for export in France and on "Lilac Island" in the Aalsmeer region of the Netherlands.

Peonies are at their best when they are fully open, which takes two to four days. Buy or pick unopened buds well ahead of time.

6 to 8 stems double lilacs (or 12 to 15 stems single bloom variety)
3 peonies
6 tulips
2¹/₂ yards 1¹/₄-inch-wide wired satin ribbon
vinyl tape
24-gauge cloth-covered wire
corsage pin

Make this bouquet the day before the wedding.

Groom the flowers, removing all the leaves, and any bruised or brown florets or petals.

Lay one lilac on a work surface. Place a peony at the base of the lilac, covering the lilac stem.

Add lilacs one at a time, to form a diamond shape. The stems will form the handle.

Place the peonies and tulips alternately on top of the lilacs, layering them so that no stems show.

Tape the stems together as close to the flower heads as possible.

Trim the stem handle to 5 inches, and cut a 1-inch slit up the woody stems of the lilacs to allow them to absorb water.

Put the bouquet into a container of water, mist it, cover it loosely with a plastic bag, and store it in the refrigerator.

With 1¹/₂ yards of the ribbon, make a six-loop bow and wire the center (page 108).

Dry the stems thoroughly andwire the bow to the base of the bouquet.

To finish, cover the handle with the remaining ribbon, and secure it with a corsage pin under the bow.

May

Wearing a veil at your wedding is a custom that came from the Far East, where the veils brides wore were red. To thwart kidnappers on their way to the ceremony, the women of the bridal party covered their heads and faces with veils and dressed alike to disguise the one who held the dowry-purse.

There are many superstitions about the bridal veil. If you mind them, you will always be lucky:

- You'll always have money if you marry in your grandmother's veil.
- Put your veil on after your last look in the mirror.
- Your veil must be placed on your head by a happily married woman.
- Drape the veil over your face so the first person to see you married is your husband.
- Make sure to tear the veil a bit at the wedding.
- And never, never wear the veil after your wedding day.

Necklace

LILY OF THE VALLEY:
Sweetness
Return of Happiness

The sweet-smelling lily of the valley, or "ladder to heaven," is dedicated to Ostara, the Norse goddess of the dawn and springtime. A Dutch bride will carry them in her bouquet, and later she and her husband will plant lily of the valley pips in their garden together. The couple will celebrate their love again when the flowers return on their first anniversary.

These stems of tiny bell-like flowers announce the return of May and, happily, warm weather.

10 stems lily of the valley
18 inches jewelry wire (available in bead shops)
light green florist tape

Make this necklace the night before the wedding.

Groom the lily of the valley, removing the leaves and any wilted or bruised flowers. Cut each stem off just under the bottom flower.

Cut four pieces of tape 5 inches long. Cut each piece in half lengthwise to make narrow strips.

Select a lily of the valley with several flowers at the tip. Carefully thread one end of the wire into the stem, taking care not to pierce the stem.

Lay another flower, overlapping the first, and carefully tape to the wire. Use very little tape and hide it as much as you can with the next flower.

Taping as you work, add flowers until half the wire is covered.

Repeat the process starting at the other end of the wire.

Mist the necklace, and refrigerate it in a loose plastic bag.

Before draping the necklace around the bride's neck, gently shake off any excess water. Bend the wire into place if necessary.

Wedding Bells

LILY OF THE VALLEY: Delicate Simplicity, Purity The lily of the valley bouquet is a favorite of celebrity brides—Elizabeth Taylor, Barbra Streisand, Brooke Shields, and Carolyn Bessette Kennedy; White House brides—Eleanor Wilson and Trisha Nixon; and royal brides—Princess Grace of Monaco and Princess Diana.

60 stems lily of the valley
2 yards 2$^{1}/_{2}$-inch-wide silk ribbon
vinyl tape
6 corsage pins

Make this bouquet the night before the wedding.

Separate the flowers from the leaves. Set aside twelve unblemished leaves.

Put the straight-stemmed flowers in a glass of water.

Place the curved stems around the rim of another glass, each one pointing away from the center, making a circle.

Put the straight stems of lily of the valley inside the circle of curved ones.

Take the bouquet out of the glass and tape the stems together.

Add the leaves around the bouquet. Tape in place.

Put the bouquet in a container of water, mist it well.

Cover the bouquet with a loose plastic bag, and store it in the refrigerator.

Shortly before the wedding, remove the bouquet from the water and dry the stem handle thoroughly.

Cover the handle with ribbon.

Fold the end of the ribbon under and secure it with a row of pins.

With the remaining ribbon tie a bow on the handle in the front of the bouquet.

Diane's Garden

ROSE: Love

BRIDAL ROSE: Happy Love

WHITE ROSEBUD: Worthiness
Purity

Throughout history roses have been unquestionably the most-favored flower. Paintings of roses decorated the walls of Egyptian palaces. The Romans adorned statues of their gods with garlands of roses and rained rose petals over their celebrations. Early Christians condemned the rose as a symbol of paganism and lust, but the people would not abandon them. Nearly a thousand years later, Pope Leo IX consecrated the rose to the Virgin Mary.

Many varieties of garden roses make exquisite bouquets for bride and attendants. These creamy white roses tinged with pale pink are called "Honor." The rosy-edged "Sheer Bliss" from my mother's garden are also called bridal roses because they are so well suited for bouquets. They have hearty stems and beautiful pointed blooms, and their white petals are blushed with pink to complement the bride's complexion.

3 small branches lemon leaves
20 garden roses
2 yards 3-inch-wide picot-edged ribbon
dark green florist tape

Make this bouquet the day before the wedding.

Remove the lemon leaves from the branches. Select 20 of the most perfect leaves. Wash and dry them. Set aside.

Groom the roses, removing the leaves and thorns.

Tape the bottom of a lemon leaf to each rose stem about 2 inches below the flower.

To make the bouquet, start with one rose and leaf, then add others, one at a time in a spiral with the leaves pointing out from the center.

Tape the stems together securely just under the flowers. Trim the stems evenly across the bottom.

Put the bouquet into a container of water, mist it, cover it with a loose plastic bag, and refrigerate overnight.

Shortly before the wedding, remove the bouquet from the water and dry the stems thoroughly.

To finish, tie a big bow over the tape, leaving the natural stems showing.

Sweetheart

PINK ROSE: Perfect Happiness

At a Polish wedding, sugar is sprinkled on the bouquet to keep the bride sweet-tempered.

15 medium roses
36 stems miniature roses
1 yard 1½-inch-wide decorative-edged ribbon
floral foam bouquet holder with
slanted handle (page 107)

Make this bouquet the day before the wedding.
Soak the bouquet holder in cool water until no
  air bubbles appear.
Groom the medium roses, removing the leaves
  and thorns. Cut the stems to 2½ inches.
Put the bouquet holder into a heavy container
  so you can use both hands to apply the flowers.
Arrange the medium roses around the edge of the holder by
  pushing the stems into the foam, the flowers facing away

away from the center. Place the most pointed
  rose at the bottom to make the point of the
  heart shape. Leave a space in the center of the
  top to make the indentation of the heart.
Groom the miniature roses, leaving a few buds
  and tiny leaves. Cut the stems to 1½ inches.
Push the stems of the miniature roses into the
  foam, filling in the heart and completely
  covering the foam.
Mist the bouquet lightly, cover with a loose
  plastic bag, and keep in a cool place.
Shortly before the wedding, double the ribbon
  and tie a bow on the top of the handle.
To finish, pull the loops toward the bottom of the bouquet.

June

Traditionally the flower pinned to the groom's coat is plucked from the bride's bouquet, one of the first expressions of their commitment to share everything in life. The groom's flowers can be just as original and imaginative as the bride's. And they can be dried for a keepsake, too.

Top (left to right): Hydrangea and dusty miller for the groom of the Mermaid Bride (page 60),
red rose and cypress complements Evergreen (page 89), Muscari with the Tussie Mussie (page 12)
Bottom: Herbs for Elizabethan (page 50), spray rose and angel vine for Jasmin's Ruffles (page 49)

Boutonnieres

Boutonnieres for the father-of-the-bride and groomsmen should complement the attendants' bouquets. The groom's boutonniere can be made with a flower from the bride's bouquet.

Top (left to right): Heather for Beloved Cathy (page 93), dendrobium orchids and fern with Aloha (page 78)
Bottom: Tuberose and camellia leaf for Camille (page 103) and leaves for Falling Leaves (page 72)

Make the boutonnieres early on the day of the wedding.
Select one perfect flower, or a few if the blooms are small.
  (The boutonniere will look like a corsage if it is too large.)
Cut the stems 1½ inches long.
Wire the flower (pages 107-109). Trim wire to 2 inches.
Place it on top of a leaf or other small piece of greenery.

Wrap the two stems together with florist tape very neatly,
  covering the wire completely.
Curl the end of the wire around a pencil.
To finish, decorate with ribbon.
Secure the boutonniere to the man's left lapel using a
  corsage pin.

Charming

Ranunculus, "the little frog flower" (*ranu* is Latin for frog), likes to live near water. King Louis IX brought ranunculuses to his mother after the Fifth Crusade, but they did not flourish. Several hundred years later, its corms were stolen from a sultan's garden in the Ottoman Empire and traded in the Marseilles flower market.

This little bouquet is constructed with concentric rings of flowers in the Biedermeier style. It is easy to put together after the preparation is done.

4 to 5 ranunculuses
12 stems lily of the valley
18 stephanotis blossoms
4 stems tweedia
3 roses
1 yard 1-inch-wide ribbon
18 wire stephanotis stems (page 107)
white florist tape
24-gauge cloth-covered wire
corsage pin

Make this bouquet the day before the wedding.

Groom the flowers by removing any damaged petals and all the leaves. Set aside six lily of the valley leaves.

Remove the stems from the stephanotis.

Dip the cotton tip of a stephanotis stem wire into water for about 5 seconds. From the bottom of the flower, with a twisting motion, push the cotton tip of the stem into the flowers.

Snip nine clusters of tweedia flowers from their stems and tape to two of the wired stephanotis. Set aside.

Tape together six stems of lily of the valley just below the flowers.

Place ranunculuses around the lily of the valley, covering the tape. Add roses, spaced evenly just below the ranunculuses.

Surround the roses with the tweedia and stephanotis clusters, bending the wires so you create an even circle. Tape.

Fold the lily of the valley leaves in half and tape them under the stephanotis, covering the wires, and tape.

Place the stems of the remaining lily of the valley between the leaves so the flowers are exposed. Tape to stem handle.

Put the bouquet into a container of water, mist lightly, cover loosely with a plastic bag, and store in the refrigerator.

Shortly before the wedding, remove the bouquet from the water and dry the stems thoroughly. Trim the stems neatly. To finish, cover handle with the ribbon and secure it with a corsage pin.

Pleasure

SWEET PEA: Delicate, Blissful, and Lasting Pleasures   The delirious scent of sweet peas delighted English gardeners when they were brought from Sicily three hundred years ago. The sweet pea became the floral symbol of Edwardian England and graced every dinner party table, tussie mussie, and bridal bouquet. Three hundred years of commercial cultivation has bred sweet peas in an array of colors, but sadly most have lost their heavenly perfume.

30 stems sweet peas
2 peonies
10 tulips
10 stems freesia
12 stems lisianthus
1 yard 1-inch-wide ribbon
2 yards 4-inch-wide silk ribbon
vinyl tape
corsage pin

Make this bouquet the day before the wedding.

Clean and groom all the flowers, removing the leaves and any bruised or damaged petals.

Make a 10-inch-long crescent-shaped bouquet of 20 sweet peas by placing them in your hand one at a time and arranging them evenly.

Place the two peonies near the stem end of the bouquet.

Tape the peony and the sweet pea stems together.

Add tulips and freesia alternately to the bouquet, allowing the natural curve of their stems to conform to the crescent.

Tape the stems in place.

Fill spaces in the bouquet with lisianthus and the remaining sweet peas.

Trim the stems to 5 inches.

Put the bouquet into a container of water. Mist lightly. (Do not mist heavily because this can cause spots on the sweet peas.) Cover the bouquet loosely with a plastic bag, and keep in a cool place.

Shortly before the wedding, remove the bouquet from the water and dry the stems thoroughly. Wrap the handle of the bouquet with the 1-inch ribbon. Secure it with a corsage pin.

Use the 4-inch-wide ribbon to tie a big bow with streamers around the handle.

To finish, trim the streamers with pinking shears.

Joy

GARDENIA: Joy
Secret Love

Since the Middle Ages, in the mountains of Austria and Germany, considerate men have presented their betrothed with a bride's box. Usually oval-shaped and made of wood, the delicate boxes are painted with flowers, birds, and messages of love. The box originally was meant to hold the private possessions and personal treasures of the bride-to-be when the rest of her belongings, like she herself, became the property of her husband.

Gardenias are particularly loved for their sensuous fragrance. Handle them carefully and only by their stems since they will bruise wherever you touch the petals. Covered and refrigerated, gardenias will stay fresh for days.

10 gardenias
5 yards 1¹/₂-inch-wide wired ribbon
24-gauge white-cloth-covered wire
white florist tape
tissue paper

This bouquet may be made early on the day before the wed-
    ding. It is not difficult to make, but it is time-consuming.
Cut a 30-inch piece of ribbon. Set aside.
Cut the remaining ribbon into ten 15-inch pieces.
Cut wire into eighteen 8-inch pieces and four 18-inch pieces.
From the ten 15-inch pieces of ribbon make simple bows and
    attach an 8-inch piece of wire to the center of each bow.
Remove the gardenia flowers from their stems.
Using 8-inch wires, wire and tape 8 gardenias.
Wire another gardenia to an 18-inch piece of wire, and wrap
    with tape. Lay a bow on the wire just under the edge of the
    flower and tape it in place.
With another 18-inch wire, start with a bow, then add a
    wired gardenia, then another bow, and another wired gar-
    denia, taping as you apply each.
Wire a gardenia to a third 18-inch wire, then add a bow, a
    wired gardenia, a bow, and another wired gardenia.
Finally, starting with a bow, attach four gardenias and four
    bows to the last 18-inch wire.
Carefully, so you do not bruise the gardenias, gather the
    wires together.
Place the wire with four flowers in the center and the others
    to the sides to make an asymmetrical bouquet.

Twist one of the wires around the others to create a handle.
    Trim the wires evenly. Cover the handle with a generous
    amount of tape.
Mist the bouquet lightly and cover with a loose plastic bag.
    Lay the bouquet on a shelf in the refrigerator on several
    pieces of wrinkled tissue paper to cushion it.
Shortly before the wedding, remove the bouquet from
    the refrigerator.
Bend the handle behind the flowers. To finish, double the
    30-inch piece of ribbon and tie into a bow at the top of
    the handle.

July

Many Europeans include herbs in their marriage rituals. A German mother-of-the-bride puts dill and salt in her daughter's shoe to protect her from evil spirits. A Czech bridesmaid may make a small bouquet of rosemary and pin it to the lapel of the single man she wishes will escort her to the wedding. The maid of honor weaves a crown of rosemary for the bride. In France, bay laurel leaves are still scattered on the path to the church.

In ancient times brides carried fragrant and flowering herbs for protection from jealous evil spirits and to guard against the threat of trolls. A bouquet of herbs was held to ensure that the couple would enjoy good fortune, happiness, and many children.

Heaven

These sapphire to sky-blue star-shaped flowers have been cultivated since the time of the pharaohs. They are sometimes called larkspur or belladonna, but it is because of the dolphin shape of the unopened flower that the delphinium get its true name, which comes from the Greek *delphis*, meaning "dolphin."

3 stems delphinium
24 stems red sweet peas
36 to 48 stems white sweet peas
1 yard 1-inch-wide white ribbon
1 yard 4-inch-wide ribbon
white florist tape
24-gauge cloth-covered wire
corsage pin

Make this bouquet the night before the wedding.

Carefully pick 24 of the best delphinium blossoms from their stems. Using florist tape, attach each blossom to a 9-inch piece of wire. Cover the wire with tape. Set aside.

Groom the sweet peas, removing the leaves and wilted or bruised flowers.

Place the red sweet peas evenly around the edge of a container (page 110).

Add rows of white sweet peas inside the circle of red ones, working in circles toward the center.

Thread the wired delphiniums through the bouquet randomly so they appear to hover just above the sweet peas.

Lift the bouquet from the container. Adjust the flowers into an oval shape. Tape the stems together.

Trim the stems and put the bouquet into water. Mist. (Do not mist heavily because this can cause spots on the sweet peas.)

Shortly before the wedding, remove the bouquet from the water and carefully dry the stems.

Wind the 1-inch-wide ribbon around the stems to form a handle. Secure with a corsage pin.

To finish, double the 4-inch-wide ribbon and tie a fat four-loop bow at the top of the handle.

Jasmin's Ruffles

GODETIA: Revealing

ANGEL VINE: Intoxication

Godetia is a flower native to California. Its showy blossoms, like ruffled ribbons, fill the garden after the last spring bulbs have gone and before the arrival of the first blooms of summer. In Germany this flower is called *Sommerazalee* and in England its common name is, appropriately, "farewell to spring." Angel vine is sometimes called "mattress vine." It climbs on a host tree and can be bought as a potted plant or topiary.

20 stems godetia
36 spray roses
15 strands angel vine, 8 to 12 inches long
green vinyl tape
1 yard 1½-inch-wide cotton ribbon

Make this bouquet the day before the wedding.

Clean the godetia stems of leaves and unopened buds. Strip the roses of all leaves, thorns, and most of the unopened buds.

Gather 12 roses into a circle, flat on top, rather than dome-shaped.

Tape the stems together securely.

Add 10 strands of the vine, placing them evenly around the circle of roses. Make loops from some of the vines. Tuck one end in among the roses and tape the other end of the vine to the rose stems.

Place the godetia around the roses and vines, creating a ruffle of godetia blossoms. Tape them in place as you work.

Add the remaining roses in a circle behind and under the godetia flowers to hide their stems. Tape the roses in place.

Arrange the remaining vines around the outside edge of the bouquet and secure with tape.

Cut the stems off squarely across the bottom, creating a handle that is 6 inches long.

Put the bouquet into water in a cool place.

Before the wedding thoroughly dry the stem handle, then wrap it with ribbon, and tie a neat bow at the top.

Elizabethan

BASIL: Good Wishes
Serious Intentions

BAY: Glory

CHAMOMILE: Comfort
Gentleness

OREGANO: Happiness
Joy

ROSEMARY: Remembrance
Fidelity

SAGE: Wisdom; Longevity

THYME: Courage
Enjoyment

1. Rosemary 2. Flowering Oregano 3. Lemon Balm 4. Bay Laurel 5. Flowering Thyme 6. Ladies mantle 7. Sage 8. Culinary Oregano 9. Oregano 10. Lavender 11. Basil 12. German Chamomile 13. Wood Sage 14. Lavender 15. Winter Savory

The herbs in this bouquet were picked at Green Gulch Farm, an organic garden near the ocean in northern California. You may find herbs for your bouquet in a friend's kitchen garden, or fresh cut at your local farmer's market; or you could grow your own in pots in a sunny window. You can be flexible in your choice of herbs, but remember that chives and dill wilt quickly and will look rather sad.

Elizabethan brides carried little bunches of fragrant dill and lavender and marigolds washed in rosewater. Sage, chives, thyme, and oregano all produce darling flowers for a summer bouquet. Any herbs you include will honor ancient tradition bringing luck and delicious scents to your wedding.

8 sprigs sage
8 clusters basil
18 stems lavender (two varieties)
8 stems winter savory
30 to 40 German chamomile flowers
8 stems flowering thyme
10 stems flowering oregano (two varieties)
5 stems flowering culinary oregano
4 stems ladies mantle
5 stems rosemary
8 stems wood sage
2 stems lemon balm
2 sprigs bay laurel
wet cotton and plastic wrap
24-gauge cloth-covered wire
light green florist tape
1 yard 1-inch-wide natural linen ribbon
corsage pin

This bouquet requires a lot of time so it should be made early on the day before the wedding.

Groom the herbs, removing any brown or bruised leaves and flowers. Clean the stems.

Using the smaller herbs—sage, basil, the smaller variety of lavender, savory, chamomile flowers, and flowering thyme—make 8 small clusters of herbs, layered according to their size, with the smallest on top. Tape the stems of each cluster together.

Snip the stems in each cluster to an even length. Wrap the cut ends with a small piece of wet cotton. Cover the cotton with a small piece of plastic wrap, and tape it around the stems to keep the cut ends wet and the herbs fresh.

Gently wrap the end of each cluster with one end of an 10-inch piece of wire. Cover the plastic wrap and the wire with florist tape. Set the clusters of herbs aside.

Since this bouquet is to be held horizontally in the bride's right hand, construct it while looking into a mirror, with the herbs held in your right hand.

Begin with the herbs that have the longest stems—flowering oregano, ladies mantle, and lavender. Add them one at a time, forming a crescent-shaped bouquet.

Next add the rosemary, wood sage, lemon balm, and bay laurel leaves.

As you add the herbs tape the stems together to form a handle.

Tuck the wired herb clusters in close to the handle and into the body of the bouquet, taking care to fill any bare spaces.

Adjust the position of each cluster as you build a plump crescent-shaped bouquet. The herbs should appear to shower from the handle.

Tape the cluster wires to the handle. Clip the wires and the stems to equal length.

Mist the bouquet well then place it in a loose plastic bag, and keep it in the refrigerator overnight.

Shortly before the wedding, cover the handle neatly with the ribbon. Secure the ribbon in place with a corsage pin.

August

Venus, the goddess of love and beauty, is a guest at every wedding. Long before the rise of Rome, she tended to the beauty of orderly nature. She was the guardian of vineyards and the protector of kitchen gardens. This goddess will be present in her special wedding gifts of flowers, wine, and sensual love.

Twice-kissed

LOVE-IN-A-MIST: Twice-kissed; Perplexity

Love-in-a-mist has a most appealing and descriptive name. The French found the tiny hairlike leaves entwined in its white blossoms provocative and named the flower *chevaux de Venus*, "hairs of Venus." In Egypt its tiny black seeds are baked into cakes and eaten by brides to gain weight because a plump woman is considered more seductive than a thin one.

15 pincushions (scabiosa)
24 love-in-a-mist
1 gerbera daisy
six 9-inch diameter tulle rounds (page 107)
3 yards 5-inch-wide tulle ribbon
24-gauge cloth-covered wire
light green florist tape
corsage pin

Make this bouquet the day before the wedding.
Groom the flowers, removing any bruised or wilted petals.
Wire the pincushion stems with 9-inch lengths of wire (pages 107-108).
Starting with the gerbera, make a free-form bouquet by adding the pincushions and love-in-a-mist stems one at a time. Vary the height of the flower heads for a three-dimensional effect.
Tape the stems together, and trim them.
Place the bouquet in an upright container, mist it lightly, cover with a loose plastic bag, and refrigerate.
Cut an X 1-inch by 1-inch in the center of each tulle circle.
Before the wedding, remove the bouquet from the refrigerator.
Pull the stems through the X in the tulle circles.
Wrap the stems with the tulle ribbon, tying a fat bow at the top.
To finish, separate, and fluff the layers of tulle.

Lucia's Lace

Wild carrot flowers are named for the virtuous Queen Anne, the last of the Stuarts to rule England. She wore a frilly cap of lace that reminded her people of this common field flower. Anne married Prince George of Denmark and had seventeen children. During her reign in the early eighteenth century, Queen Anne established the first English public garden at Kensington Palace.

9 Lucia roses
6 stems green amaranthus
24 stems Queen Anne's lace
2 yards 3-inch-wide double-faced satin ribbon
24-gauge cloth-covered wire
light green florist tape
corsage pins

Make this bouquet the day before the wedding.

Groom the roses, removing the leaves and thorns, and wire the stems (page 107-109).

Cut the amaranthus tendrils off their stems. Put the cut ends together to form a loop. Twist one end of a 9-inch piece of wire around the ends and secure it with florist tape. Make approximately a dozen wired loops, and set them aside.

Make 8 clusters of Queen Anne's lace, with three flowers in each. Trim the stems to about 8 inches. Set aside.

Arrange the roses in three rows of three to form a square. Tape the stems.

Place two clusters of Queen Anne's lace on each side of the rose square. Secure with florist tape.

Arrange the wired amaranthus loops around the bouquet, tucking them just under the Queen Anne's lace, so they hang like swag fringe.

Tape the wires neatly to the stem handle. Trim the handle to a point.

Mist the bouquet well, and store in the refrigerator.

Shortly before the wedding, wrap the handle tightly with $1/2$ yard of the ribbon. Secure the ribbon in place with a corsage pin.

To finish, tie the remaining ribbon in a soft bow at the top of the handle.

Marsha's Heart

DAISY: Innocence and Simplicity
Faith and Cheer

IVY: Fidelity, Wedded Love

Chaucer called daisies *eie of daie* because they open with the sunrise. Old superstitions claim that if a girl puts daisies under her pillow she will dream of her true love, and a daisy placed in the bride's left stocking will assure an early pregnancy. I carried daisies, a symbol of peace for my generation, when I was married at the age of eighteen. The daisy represents the qualities of a young bride—innocent and filled with faith—her eyes wide open.

60 daisies
2 to 4 12-inch-lengths ivy
2 yards 1-inch-wide satin ribbon
floral foam bouquet holder with slanted handle (page 107)
24-gauge cloth-covered wire
corsage pin

The foam in the holder will keep the daisies fresh if this bouquet is made the day before the wedding.

Soak the holder in cool water until no air bubbles appear. Place the holder in a heavy container to hold it upright so you can use both hands to apply the flowers.

Cut 24 of the daisy stems to 3 inches, and strip off the leaves. Push the daisy stems into the foam, facing away from the center to create a heart-shaped outline of overlapping flowers. Cut the stems shorter where the heart indents in the center of the top edge, and use some flowers with longer stems to make the bottom point.

Add a second row of overlapping daisies on the inside of the heart outline.

Cut the stems of the remaining daisies to 2 to 2$\frac{1}{2}$ inches. Strip off the leaves. Fill in the heart, completely covering the foam with daisies.

Cut four 3-inch pieces of wire, and bend them like hairpins.

Using a bent wire, secure one end of an ivy stem to the top center of the heart. (If the ivy does not have enough leaves, twist it with another strand for more fullness.)

Pull the ivy around the outside edge of the bouquet, and secure it at the bottom point with another bent wire, leaving a few leaves dangling.

Repeat on the opposite side.

Mist the bouquet well, and refrigerate overnight.

Shortly before the wedding, wrap the handle of the holder neatly with ribbon, and secure with a corsage pin.

September

A bride in the Victorian Age carried a bouquet made from several small clusters of flowers. After the ceremony she presented a little bouquet to each of her attendants. Hidden in one was a small gold ring that assured the lucky bridesmaid that she would be the next woman to marry.

Mermaid Bride

HYDRANGEA: Devotion Victorian ladies embellished the bridal bouquet with trinkets of sentimental value—a cameo or pendant, seashells or feathers, ribbons, and pretty buttons. They made flowers from silk, paper, beads, and sometimes from a lock of their beloved's hair. My version has flowers my sisters and I made from glass beads and seashells we collected at the beach.

1 dusty miller plant
7 to 10 white lacecap hydrangea flowers
2 dozen faux pearl sprays (page 107)
10 bead flowers on wires
6 seashell flowers on wires
10 seashells on wires
(You can substitute earrings or other costume jewelry,
hair clips, or beaded flowers taped to a wire.)
3 yards 2-inch-wide ivory double-faced satin ribbon
3 yards 1-inch-wide white double-faced satin ribbon
3 yards $^1/_2$-inch-wide white picot-edged
double-faced satin ribbon
5 yards $^1/_4$-inch-wide ivory satin ribbon
5 yards $^1/_4$-inch-wide white satin ribbon
white florist tape
vinyl tape
21-gauge wire
corsage pins

Make this bouquet the night before the wedding.
Clip leaves from the dusty miller plant. Attach a 9-inch wire
to the base of each leaf and cover wire with florist tape.

Remove leaves and bruised or dried florets from the
hydrangeas.
Make clusters using one hydrangea, a seashell, one or two
bead flowers, and two faux pearl sprays in each one. Vary
the placement so that some shells and bead flowers hover
above the hydrangea and others nestle among the florets.
Tape the wires to the hydrangea stems.
Gather the clusters, gently placing them close together to
form the shape you like. Tape the stems together with vinyl
tape, and trim them evenly.
Mist the hydrangea, then add the dusty miller leaves around
the bouquet, hiding the backs of the hydrangeas.
Place the bouquet in water. Keep in a cool place.
Shortly before the wedding, dry the stems and cover them
neatly with the 2-inch-wide ivory satin ribbon. Secure with
a corsage pin.
Cut the remaining ribbon into lengths of 36 to 60 inches.
Put the centers of the ribbons together and tie them in a
bow. Twist a wire around the center of the bow, and attach
it to the top of the handle so the streamers hang from the
bottom of the front of the bouquet.

Mermaid of Honor

WHITE ROSE: Girlhood
Innocence

The Honor Attendant deserves a bouquet reflecting her meaningful place at the side of the bride. She is chosen to tend to the train and veil, hold the bridal bouquet while rings are given, and sign as a witness to the marriage. Married or maiden, she stands up for her sister or best friend on her wedding day.

12 white baby roses
5 or 6 blue and green hydrangeas
12 crystal sprays (page 107)
10 bead flowers
2¹⁄₂ yards ¹⁄₂-inch-wide wired ribbon
1¹⁄₂ yards ³⁄₄-inch-wide wired sheer ribbon
21-gauge wire
vinyl tape
light green florist tape
corsage pin

Make this bouquet the day before the wedding.

Remove the leaves and thorns from the roses and wire the stems (pages 107-109). Using florist tape, attach a crystal spray to each rose.

Gather the hydrangea flowers together, and arrange them in an oval bouquet, placing the green flowers on the bottom.

Thread the roses and the bead flowers through the hydrangeas.

Tape the stems together. Cut the stems across the bottom so they are even. Mist them well with water.

Put the bouquet in a container of water in a cool place.

Shortly before the wedding, remove the bouquet from the water, and dry the stems thoroughly.

Wrap the stems with the ¹⁄₂-inch-wide wired ribbon, and secure it with a corsage pin.

Double the remaining ribbon, and tie it securely around the handle at the top.

To finish, cut the streamers to varying lengths, then curl them around your fingers.

La Linda

DAHLIA: Elegance; Dignity; Forever Yours   Montezuma II had palace gardens unrivaled by any court in Europe. When the Spaniards invaded Mexico, Cortes' men were astonished by the fabulous array of dahlias—flowers they had never seen before. When they were smuggled into Spain, these gorgeous blooms became so popular with Europeans that one tuber was traded for a diamond; and a prize of one thousand pounds was offered for a single blue dahlia. The prize was never claimed.

The stems of these flamboyant sunburst blooms are rigid, but delicate. They are not easy to work with, but the amazing flowers and extraordinary array of colors, abundant size, and multitude of varieties make them well worth the effort.

12 dahlias of various colors and sizes
10 stems lemon leaves
3 yards $1^1/_4$-inch-wide wired satin ribbon
($1^1/_2$ yards each of colors complemetary to your dahlias)
21-gauge wire
light green florist tape
vinyl tape
corsage pins

Make this bouquet the night before the wedding.

Wire the stems of the dahlias gently, turning the wire around each stem only once (pages 107-108).

Arrange the smaller dahlias around the largest one, crossing the stems over each other, so they make an hourglass shape. Do not bend these stems because they crush easily.

Gently pull the large center dahlia higher than the surrounding flowers to create a pointed dome-shaped bouquet.

When you are satisfied with the placement of the flowers and the shape of the bouquet, use vinyl tape to attach the wired stems together, beginning at the narrow part and taping down to the end of the stems.

Add a row of lemon leaves around and under the outside edge of the bouquet, covering any visible stems, wires, and spaces between the dahlias. Tape in place.

Trim the stems evenly, leaving a 5-inch handle.

Put the bouquet in a container of water, and keep in a cool place.

Shortly before the wedding, remove the bouquet from the water, and dry the stems thoroughly.

Cover the handle with ribbon. Pin the ribbon securely in place.

Double the remaining ribbon, and tie it around the top of the handle in a loose bow.

To finish, curl the streamers around your fingers, and let them cascade down from the front of the handle.

Sunshine

SUNFLOWER: Adoration

BLACK-EYED SUSAN: Justice

COREOPSIS: Gladness

A mortal woman named Clytie fell passionately in love with Helios, the Greek god of the sun. She stared at him throughout the day, following his journey across the sky. Helianthus, the "sunflower," like the adoring Clytie, faces the sun from dawn to dusk.

6 medium-sized sunflowers
6 orange sunflowers
5 to 6 black-eyed Susans
18 coreopsis
2$\frac{1}{2}$ yards 1$\frac{1}{4}$-inch-wide wired satin ribbon
21-gauge wire
vinyl tape
corsage pins

Make this bouquet the night before the wedding.

Clean all the stems, and remove any dry or bruised petals from the flowers.

Start with one sunflower facing straight up, then place the other five sunflowers around it facing out, petals touching.

When you have the sunflowers evenly arranged, tape them together firmly, covering about 3 inches of the stems, to make a covered handle. If the sunflower stems are very thick, cut away some of their bulk with a sharp knife, and cover well with the tape.

Thread the black-eyed Susans, orange sunflowers, and six of the coreopsis between the sunflowers at varying levels, filling any spaces. Tape the stems to the handle.

Arrange the remaining coreopsis around the underside of the bouquet to hide the sunflower stems. Tape to handle.

Trim the handle to 7 inches. Put the bouquet in a container of water, and store in the refrigerator.

Shortly before the wedding, remove the bouquet from the vase, and dry the stems thoroughly. Trim 2 inches from the stems, then wrap the stems with ribbon and pin it securely as close to the bouquet as possible.

To finish, make a loose bow with the remaining ribbon, and wire it to the top of the handle.

October

Chrysanthemums, autumn leaves, and asters adorned with ribbons and lace grace the bride in the golden fall. The chrysanthemum shares the same Chinese character with autumn and is the symbol for the greatest gifts bestowed upon the wife and husband—good health and longevity.

Fan for Kim

AMARANTHUS: Abundant Harvest; Immortality; Unfading Love
CHRYSANTHEMUM: "Golden Flower"; Loveliness Asian brides carry a special fan, often decorated with gold, instead of a bouquet. To honor two cultural traditions, a bride may carry a fan adorned with flowers. Yellow chrysanthemums and a fringe of gold amaranthus, an edible grain, ensures long life and prosperity.

10 stems gold amaranthus
6 yellow Football chrysanthemums
1 yard 1¹/₂-inch-wide ribbon
2 fans, one miniature
24-gauge cloth-covered wire

Make this flower decoration the night before the ceremony.
Groom the chrysanthemums, and cut the stems to 9 inches.
Facing a mirror, hold the amaranthus by the stems in one hand. Arrange the amaranthus tendrils so they are evenly spaced, pointing toward the front, and hanging downward like fringe.

Add the chrysanthemums in a row above the hanging amaranthus. Keep the back side of the bouquet as flat as possible.
Pull a few amaranthus tendrils between the chrysanthemums.
Trim the stems to a 4- to 5-inch handle and wrap them with the wire.
Mist the bouquet, and refrigerate overnight.
Shortly before the wedding, attach the miniature fan to a piece of wire about 8 inches long. Thread the wire between the flowers, and secure it to the back of the bouquet.
Cover the handle with ribbon.
Bend an 8-inch piece of wire in half, and thread it between the slats from the back of the fan. Secure it to the handle.

Emi's Chatelaine

WHITE
CHRYSANTHEMUM: Absolute
Truth

ASTER: Daintiness; Patience

A chatelaine is traditionally a round or oval bouquet trimmed with long ribbons tied into little lovers' knots. These enormous and elaborate ribbon-festooned bouquets were a favorite of American brides at the turn of the twentieth century. The lovers' knots on the ribbons have special meanings: two knots on one ribbon symbolize the joining of a man and a woman; three knots represents man, woman, and child.

24 stems pom-pom chrysanthemums
10 Football chrysanthemums
24 Matsumoto asters
raffia
10 yards $1/2$-inch-wide picot-edged ribbon
21-gauge wire

Make this bouquet the day before the wedding.

Groom all the flowers. Trim the stems to 10 inches.

In your hand, criss-cross the stems of the chrysanthemums and of ten asters, arranging the flowers so they create an oval-shaped bouquet. To create depth and dimension, vary the height of the flowers so they are not all on one level.

When you are pleased with the arrangement, trim the stems evenly and wrap the bottom half of the stems (below the point where they criss-cross) with raffia. Tie securely.

Put the bouquet into a container of water, mist it well, and put it in a cool place.

Cut the ribbon into various lengths from 24- to 40-inches. Fold the ribbons in half, and put the centers of the ribbons together. Attach a wire at the center. Tie the ribbons in a knot around the wire.

Make two or three lovers' knots in each length of ribbon (page 111).

Shortly before the wedding, cut the stems of the remaining asters to $1^1/_2$ inches. Tie each aster on a ribbon with a lovers' knot.

Remove the bouquet from the water and dry stems thoroughly.

Anchor the ribbon wire to the back of the bouquet. Thread a few ribbons between the flowers so they dangle from the front of the bouquet, as well as hanging from the bottom.

Falling Leaves

POPLAR: Time

SYCAMORE: Curiosity

OAK: Bravery; Hospitality

ELM: Dignity

MAPLE: Reserve

According to the Chinese calendar, the red maple leaf represents October. The glorious leaves of autumn in an infinite variety of shapes and vibrant colors—yellow poplar, red maple, purple plum, brown oak, and the green and crimson of liquid amber—celebrate the lasting virtues represented by trees.

A few days before the ceremony, collect the leaves. They should be without spots or flaws, picked from the trees, not from the ground.

35 to 50 autumn leaves in a variety of colors and sizes
1 large white Football chrysanthemum
36 stems white pom-pom chrysanthemums
12 stems gold miniature Funray chrysanthemums
2$\frac{1}{2}$ yards 2-inch-wide wired double-faced satin ribbon
21-gauge wire
olive green florist tape
corsage pins
fabric glue

Press the leaves flat, stems attached, between two
sheets of craft paper or drawing paper,
then cover with heavy books.
Make 10 leaf clusters by stacking three to five
different kinds of leaves, the largest one on
the bottom. Tape the stems together. Then
tape each leaf cluster to a 9-inch piece of wire.
Set aside.
The day before the wedding, make the bouquet.
Groom the chrysanthemums and cut the stems to about
10 inches.
Start with the big chrysanthemum in the center, and circle
it with rows of white pom-pom chrysanthemums.
As you work, randomly add a few of the stems of miniature
gold chrysanthemums. Tape the stems together securely, and trim the stems
to a point.
Mist the bouquet well, put it into a container of water,
and keep it in a cool place.
Shortly before the wedding, remove the bouquet from the
water and dry the stems thoroughly.
Add the leaf clusters around the outside edge of the
bouquet. Tape the wires to the handle, and trim them.
Cover the pointed handle with ribbon. Pin the ribbon
securely in place.
With the remaining ribbon, make a bow of four big
loops and two hanging streamers. Secure center
with wire.
Using fabric glue, attach a few small
leaves
to the streamers.

November

The white wedding dress has been popular since the early nineteenth century when proper young ladies wore the fashionable chemise made of muslin, a fine white cloth imported from India. Well-to-do brides had silk and tinsel embroidery, beads, and ruffles sewn on their dresses. Those of moderate means had a plainer version, but the popular color was still white. Queen Victoria, absolute monarch of social code and correct behavior, wore white for her wedding in 1840. Brides have imitated Victoria for more than a century and a half. The dictum "white is for virginity" is a twentieth-century idea, perhaps because white symbolizes purity.

Claudia

WHEAT: Fertility
Prosperity
Abundant Harvest

Brides in ancient Rome carried sheaves of wheat to ensure fertility. At the close of the Roman marriage ceremony, bread was broken over the bride's head. The modern wedding cake, made from wheat, is a descendant of that wedding bread. It is still customary to shower the couple with grain, the symbol of riches and children that holds an eternal place in the marriage ritual.

45 stalks natural wheat
30 stalks rye wheat
10 stems fresh Walpole waxflower
2 yards $1^1/_4$-inch-wide wired silk ribbon
21-gauge wire
light green florist tape
corsage pin

Making this bouquet is very time-consuming, so begin early on the day before the wedding.

Cut the stalks of the wheat to about 4 inches.

Make a cluster, approximately the size of your hand, with one layer of three natural wheat stalks, small bunches of waxflowers, and then two rye wheat stalks. Wrap the cluster with wire, trim the excess stems, and cover the wire with tape. Make 15 clusters.

Working on a large, flat surface, start with one cluster as the bottom of the bouquet.

Add two clusters side-by-side, covering the taped end.

Taping the cluster wires together as you work, add a third row of three clusters, then a row of four clusters. Continue this way to make a cascade that is shaped like a large bunch of grapes.

Add extra small bunches of waxflowers, each taped to a wire, to fill any spaces in the bouquet.

Tape all the wires together, pick up the bouquet, and bend the wires downward behind the wheat and waxflower clusters to create handle.

Mist the bouquet well, and store it in a cool place.

Shortly before the wedding, using $1^1/_2$ yards of the ribbon, make a bow with several $3^1/_2$-inch loops. Wire the center of the bow, and attach it to the handle snug against the top clusters.

To finish, wrap the handle with the remaining ribbon, and secure it with a corsage pin.

Aloha

ORCHID: Ecstasy; Rare Beauty In medieval France, orchids were called "satyrion" after the lustful wood deities of Greek mythology. There are more than twenty-five thousand species of orchids whose name comes from the Greek *orchis*, which means "testicle." Dendrobiums are closely related to the vanilla orchid, which bears fragrant seed pods valued as an aphrodisiac throughout the southern hemisphere.

The dendrobium orchid from Hawaii is a hardy little blossom that can last more than a week, even without water. I chose this variety for its vibrant jungle green, but these beautiful orchids are also available in pale pink, white, and shades of purple.

6 stems dendrobium orchids
1 Japhette orchid
4 yards 1³/₄-inch-wide organza ribbon
²/₃ yard 1-inch-wide green velvet ribbon
24-gauge cloth-covered wire
light green florist tape

Make this bouquet the day before the wedding.
Pick the dendrobium flowers from their stems. Discard any flowers that are broken, bruised, or discolored.
Cut the wire into twelve 9-inch pieces. Bend the top 2 inches of each piece of wire to form a narrow hairpin shape.

With florist tape attach the short stems of three dendrobium flowers to the top of the wire. Make 12 of these clusters.
Gently wind wire around the stem of the Japhette orchid. Cover the wire with florist tape.
Mist the clusters and the orchid well, and refrigerate.
Cut the organza ribbon into 24-inch lengths. Fold each length twice to make a bow with four loops. Wire each bow at the center, and cover the wire with florist tape.
Shortly before the wedding, arrange one bow on either side of the Japhette orchid, and tape the wires together.
Surround the orchid and bows evenly with the dendrobium clusters. Arrange the remaining bows around the outside edge.
Trim the wire stems to form a pointed 6-inch handle. Cover well with tape.
Wrap the handle with the velvet ribbon, and finish with a small, neat bow.

Stella's Sparkle

STEPHANOTIS: Married Bliss; a Distant Journey   The exotic star-shaped stephanotis, also called Madagascar jasmine, is virginal white and has replaced orange blossoms as the favorite of brides in any month. Erotic love is suggested by the flower's enticing and subtle perfume and its ability to stay fresh through the wedding day and night.

75 stephanotis (25 to a box, special ordered from your florist)
75 stephanotis wire stems (page 107)
1¹/₂ yards rhinestone trim (page 4)
1 yard 1-inch-wide silk ribbon
4 yards 3-inch-wide wired sheer decorative ribbon
wire cutters
washable fabric glue
21-gauge wire
white florist tape

Make this bouquet early on the day before the wedding. It is not difficult to make, but it takes time.

Using wire cutters, cut seventy-five rhinestones from the trim.

Glue one rhinestone to the cotton top of each stephanotis wire stem.

Remove the green stems from the stephanotis flowers.

With a wire, poke through each flower, pushing out its green center.

Dip the cotton tip of a stem wire into water for about 5 seconds. From the bottom of the flower, with a twisting motion, push the stem into the flower until the rhinestone sits in its center. Repeat.

Cut twenty-four 8-inch pieces of wire.

Make three rhinestone-studded wired flowers into a triangle-shaped cluster. Twist an 8-inch piece of wire around the wire stems of the stephanotis and tape. Make 24 more clusters.

In your hand form a triangle-shaped bouquet of stephanotis clusters, and tape the stem wires together.

Mist the bouquet well, put it into a loose plastic bag, and keep in the refrigerator overnight.

Cut the 3-inch-wide ribbon into 24-inch lengths.

Make four 2-loop bows, and secure the centers with wire (page 108).

Shortly before the wedding, arrange the ribbon loops around the flowers, and tape the wires into place.

Trim the stem wires to a point. Cover the handle with the 1-inch-wide ribbon.

Adjust the stephanotis clusters and ribbon loops evenly to desired shape.

To finish, glue the remaining rhinestone trim to the bottom of the handle. Wind the trim in a spiral up the handle, and glue in place.

Bianca

ANTHERIUM: Attraction

ORCHID: Thoughts of You

Heart-shaped antherium, also called "flamingo flower," is native to South America. These flowers are grown in Hawaii in an amazing diversity of colors and sizes and are exported to the mainland. In this bouquet they are used like leaves behind graceful Japhette orchids.

6 Japhette orchids
6 white antherium
1 yard 2-inch-wide wired silk ribbon
white adhesive tape
21-gauge wire
white florist tape

Make this bouquet the day before the wedding.

While antherium lasts for weeks, if bent or cracked a brown line will mar the pristine white of the flower. So work with care when wiring and adjusting these flowers.

Remove the yellow spike from an antherium and cover the cut with a small piece of adhesive tape. (These turn red where cut, and if they are not covered it may show.)

From underneath the flower, very close to the stem, push one end of an 8-inch piece of wire into the adhesive tape. Repeat with each antherium.

Tuck an orchid into the V of an antherium. Tape the stems of both to the wire about 2 inches down the stem. (Do not twist the wire around the stems.) Repeat with each orchid and antherium.

Holding all the flowers by the wires, carefully arrange them into a three-dimensional diamond shape. Secure them together neatly with florist tape, leaving most of the stems exposed to make the handle.

Mist well, and store in the refrigerator.

Shortly before the wedding make a bow with several loops. Use a piece of wire to fasten the bow to the back of the bouquet.

To finish, cut the stems evenly across the bottom.

December

More American couples become engaged in December than in any other month. Christmas is the most popular day of the year for presenting an engagement ring and for beginning to make wedding plans.

According to folklore, a December marriage promises increasing love, and winter snow on your wedding day means that you will have lots of money in your future. Since Colonial times it has been considered good luck to marry on Christmas Eve since there is the likelihood that angels will attend the ceremony.

Copper Rose

ROSE: True Love; Female Beauty

Roses were sacred to Dionysus, the god of wine and revelry, and it is said that each night Nero's pillow was stuffed with fresh rose petals. When Cleopatra seduced Marc Anthony, she filled the room where she greeted him with rose petals—two feet deep. The island of Rhodes is named for the roses that grew there in abundance. On ships at sea, sailors claimed they could smell the roses on the island before sighting land.

A new rose, developed in European greenhouses, is the gold and copper-colored Leonidas. This dazzling rose is now imported to America from Ecuador and is grown in northern California hothouses.

20 Leonidas roses
9 yards 2-inch-wide green wired satin ribbon
21-gauge wire
dark green florist tape

Set aside 1 yard of ribbon to cover the handle of the bouquet. The night before the wedding prepare the roses. Cut stems to 2 inches. Wire and tape the roses with 9-inch lengths of wire (page 107-109).

Mist the roses well and store them in the refrigerator overnight. Shortly before the wedding, gather the roses in your hand, and arrange them in a dome shape. Arrange the satin leaves evenly around the bouquet and tape them in place.

Trim the wires to form a 6-inch, pointed handle. To finish, cover the handle with the reserved ribbon.

Ahead of time make 57 satin leaves. To make a leaf, fold both sides of a 5-inch piece of ribbon diagonally from the center, forming a triangle. Pinch together the bottom side of the ribbon triangle and wrap it with one end of a 9-inch wire. Cover wire with florist tape.

Kiss Me Kate

Mistletoe was prohibited in Christian churches for centuries because it was associated with pagan rites. Sacred to the Druids, mistletoe was especially important in their winter solstice celebration, and was gathered with great reverence. The Druids hung mistletoe above their doorways as a sign of peace and welcome, hence the custom of kissing under it.

Mistletoe is a parasite plant that can be found on oak and other trees. The miniature variety used in this bouquet was found growing on a branch of juniper. Remember: the berries of the mistletoe are poisonous if eaten.

18 medium-sized roses
9 large roses (those in the photograph are Bianca roses)
3 bunches of mistletoe, 1 of the miniature variety
3 yards 2^1/$_2$-inch-wide decorative ribbon
24-gauge cloth-covered wire
light green florist tape
corsage pin

Make this bouquet the night before the wedding.
Groom the roses, removing all the leaves and thorns. Wire and tape them (pages 107-109).
Cut 36 pieces of wire into 9-inch lengths.
Cut the ribbon into six 14-inch lengths. Make two loops in each and secure with a 9-inch wire.

Separate the smaller leaf mistletoe from the larger leaves. Make about 30 clusters, each about 3 inches long. Twist one end of a 9-inch wire around the cut end of each cluster.
Surround the largest rose with several clusters of the smallest mistletoe leaves. Tape together.
Make a circle of the larger roses a little under the mistletoe layer, creating a cone shape. Tape the roses in place.
Next make a circle of the larger-leafed mistletoe clusters, and tape.
Add a circle of the medium-sized roses, then tape in place.
Add a bottom layer of clusters of the largest leaf mistletoe. Secure with tape.
Arrange the ribbon loops evenly just under the bottom layer of mistletoe. Tape into place.
Trim the wires and stems on an angle into a pointed handle and cover with a gernerous amount of tape.
Wrap the handle with the remaining ribbon and secure at the top with a corsage pin to finish.
Mist the bouquet well, and store in a cool place.

Evergreen

PINE: Sympathy; Warm Friendship

SPRUCE: Hope in Adversity

FIR: Uplifting

JUNIPER: Protection

In Normandy the custom is to hold an arch of pine boughs laced with white ribbons over the groom and bride. In the Netherlands the wedding couple sits at the reception table under boughs of evergreen, symbolizing everlasting love. And in Switzerland the groom presents his bride with a decorated pine tree, which she plants in the yard of her new home. When their first child is expected, the tree is cut to make a cradle.

five 5-inch pieces noble fir
eight 6-inch pieces cedar
ten 6- to 7-inch pieces cypress
four 10-inch pieces blue spruce or blue atlas cedar
2 sprigs juniper (about the size of your hand) with berries
6 crystal snowflakes (bells, stars, or small glass
ornaments may be substituted)
1 yard 3-inch-wide double-faced satin ribbon
1 yard 1-inch-wide satin ribbon
18-gauge wire
vinyl tape

This bouquet can be made the day before the wedding.
Select a variety of fresh-cut evergreens different from each other
in color and texture. The list above recommends some.
Cut the branches in the lengths suggested above. Wrap the
cut end of each branch with wire about 1 inch up
from the bottom.
Wrap one point of each snowflake or ornament with vinyl
tape to protect it from scratches.
Cut six pieces of wire 9 inches long. Bend 2 inches at one
end of each wire, like a hairpin and, using vinyl tape, attach
it to the taped point of each ornament.
Lay out the longest wired sprigs of evergreen in a fan shape
with their wires touching. Build the bouquet by layering
the greens for contrast and definition. Add the ornaments.
Use pliers to twist all the wires together tightly to
form a handle.

Starting at the bottom, wrap the wire handle with the 1-inch
ribbon. With the 3-inch ribbon tie a bow with streamers
around the top of the handle.
Use pliers to bend the handle into a curve behind the greens.
Keep the bouquet in a cool place until the wedding.

January

Ribbons curled, pleated, braided,

shirred, twisted, tucked.

Streamers looped, draped, gathered,

tied in bows and lovers' knots.

An accessory, a memory, a complement to

the prettiest dress you've ever worn.

Consider satin, silk and organdy, damask, velvet, and tulle.

Think grosgrain, moiré, or cotton; taffeta, lace, or voile.

Choose dotted Swiss, picot-edged,

printed, striped, or plaid.

Pick embroidered, beaded, ruffled, gilded.

The perfect ribbon, extravagant perhaps, but worth it.

Beloved Cathy

HEATHER: Passion; Luck   Wild pink and purple heather blooms across the heaths and the windswept moors of the British Isles. Heather played a memorable role in the passionate love story of Cathy and Heathcliff in *Wuthering Heights*. Scottish brides have always carried heather, and in the eighteenth century newlywed emigrants brought mattresses stuffed with heather when they came to America. They planted the seeds, which took root like the couples, and brought them memories of the home they left behind.

40 stems heather
4 yards 2¹/₂-inch-wide silk ribbon
¹/₂ yard 1-inch-wide ribbon
21-gauge wire
vinyl tape

Heather will stay fresh for a long time without water, so you can make this bouquet early on the day before the wedding.

Gather 10 heather stems and cut them 4 inches from the tips. Using one end of a 9-inch length of wire, bind them together tightly in a bunch.

Double the 2¹/₂-inch-wide ribbon and tie a loose four-loop bow with two streamers onto the wired end of this miniature bouquet.

Cut the remaining stems of heather 5 inches from the tips. Make clusters of three to five stems. Make sure that each cluster comes to a graceful point.

Wrap the base of each cluster with one end of a 9-inch wire.

Pick up all the clusters and hold them by the wired ends. Thread the wired end of the miniature bouquet through the center of the clusters until it is nestled snugly into the middle.

Using a generous amount of tape, tape all the wires together tightly to form a handle. Trim the handle to 5 inches from the base of the bouquet.

Cover the handle with the 1-inch-wide ribbon.

To finish, bend the wired clusters at the top of the handle to a 45-degree angle so they fan out in a sunburst shape.

Belle Mariée & Belle Amie

ANEMONE: Protective Love

GALYX: Long-lasting Friendship

Anemone was the nymph cherished by gentle Zephyr, the Greek god of the west wind. The flower was created from his sweet breath and named for her. The anemone thrives in windy places and Europeans call it "wind flower" or "wind rose."

White anemones for *la belle mariée*, the beautiful bride, and vibrant pink for *la belle amie*, her lovely friend.

16 French anemones
12 Galyx leaves
2 yards 1¹/₂-inch-wide silk ribbon
green florist tape
corsage pin

This bouquet is so easy to make it can be done on the morning of the wedding or the night before.

Using scissors, trim all the leaves from the anemones.

Put the flowers into your hand one at a time in circles facing out from the center. After every four or five flowers, neatly tape the stems together forming the handle.

Arrange the galyx leaves so they are spaced evenly around the flowers. Tape the stems of the leaves to the handle.

Trim the stem handle straight across the bottom.

Place bouquet in water until an hour or two before the ceremony.

After you remove the bouquet from the water dry stems thoroughly.

Wind the ribbon around the handle tightly. Secure the ribbon at the top with a corsage pin.

To finish, tie the remaining ribbon in a fat bow at the top of handle.

Shining

AMARYLLIS: Splendid Beauty; Pride

The Roman poet Virgil wrote a romantic poem two thousand years ago about shepherds singing to a beautiful shepherdess named Amaryllis. Her name is derived from the Greek verb *amaryssein*, which means "to shine." Stately and splendid, the amaryllis is native to the Cape of Good Hope. It blooms in winter with spectacular white, pink or red flowers.

4 stalks amaryllis with 3 or 4 flowers on each
3 yards 1-inch-wide wired taffeta ribbon
vinyl tape

Make this bouquet the day before the wedding. Leave time to do the ribbon in the morning.

Remove the little pollen-bearing pistils from the flowers. Remove any damaged petals.

Pick up all the stalks, and move them about gently so that the flowers rest very close to each other and form a ball-shaped bouquet.

Tape the stalks together securely at the top underneath the flowers.

About 13 inches down from the flower heads, cut the stems straight across.

Put bouquet in a container of water in a cool place overnight.

Shortly before the wedding dry the stems thoroughly.

Tie the middle of the ribbon around the stems 1 inch from the cut end.

Bring the ends of the ribbon back toward the front at an angle. Wrap one around the other, then bring them both to the back and cross them.

Bring the ends back to the front again, wrap again. Continue in this way, forming a pattern of Xs all the way up the stalks.

To finish, secure with a bow at the top, covering the tape.

February

Tossing the bridal bouquet signals the end of the wedding festivities and identifies the next bride-to-be. Women have carried flowers to their nuptials since earliest days when they held a handful of herbs with magical powers to ward off evil spirits and to frighten away trolls. When the ceremony ended and there was no longer need for its protection, the bouquet was thrown in to flavor the soup for the marriage feast.

Elizabethan brides carried herbs for their aphrodisiac power; marigold washed in rosewater and sprigs of dill and lavender. The bouquet was carried to the house by the married couple and used to light the first fire in their new home. The bride then tossed the burning herbs out of her window to show the revelers it was time for them to leave.

Some would say the toss is just for luck, or to bestow a blessing. But my favorite explanation is that the bouquet is tossed into the air to distract the guests while the newlyweds make their escape.

Josephine's Memory

WHITE VIOLET: Faith; Honesty; Maidenly Modesty

SINGLE WHITE ROSE: "Don't Forget I Love You"   The modest violet was a favorite of royalty. Queen Victoria wore a violet posy every day, and her daughter-in-law, Queen Alexandra, planted five thousand violets in the gardens at Windsor Castle. Napoleon always gave violets to Josephine on their wedding anniversary. After his beloved Josephine died, he wore a locket containing violets that bloomed on her grave.

1 large white rose
3 bunches white violets with leaves
1 yard 1-inch-wide ribbon
9-inch tulle collar bouquet holder (page 107)
3 plastic sandwich bags
6 facial tissues
21-gauge wire
3 rubber bands
vinyl tape
corsage pin

Make this bouquet the night before the ceremony.

Cut one corner in a fan shape from each of the plastic bags.

Remove the leaves and thorns from the rose. Then wire it (pages 107-109) and cut the stem to 7 inches.

Keeping the violets in bunches, groom them, removing any bruised or wilted flowers.

With a sharp knife, cut the bunch of stems to a point, and wrap them with a folded tissue. Place the wrapped stems into a plastic bag. Spoon in enough water to soak the tissue. Secure the plastic bag around the stems with a rubber band. Be careful not to crush the stems.

Repeat with the other two bunches of violets.

Tape the plastic-covered stems of the violets to the rose stem so the bunches of violets surround the rose.

Mist the bouquet lightly, and place it in an upright container in the refrigerator until an hour or two before the wedding.

Shortly before the wedding, place bouquet in the holder and tape holder to the rose stem. (Before taping, you may need to cut the cone of the holder to fit the flowers properly.)

Wrap the rose stem with ribbon to make a smooth handle. Secure with a corsage pin.

Violet Posy

VIOLETS: Modesty; Faithfulness   A small bunch of flowers, usually of one variety, makes a posy. It might be wildflowers gathered on a lovers' stroll and wrapped in the lady's handkerchief for safekeeping. When carried by a bridesmaid, a little violet posy in an antique handkerchief represents modesty and her faithful friendship. It is the custom in Belgium for a bride to embroider a handkerchief with her initials, carry it at the wedding with her bouquet, and hand it on to the next bride-to-be in her family.

1

2

1. Cut one corner off the plastic bag in a fan shape. Keeping the violets in the bunch, groom them, removing any bruised or wilted flowers. With a sharp knife, cut the bunch of stems to a point.

2. Wrap the stems in a folded tissue and place them in the plastic bag. Spoon enough water into the bag to soak the tissues.
    Secure the plastic bag around the stems with a rubber band, being careful not to crush them.

This nosegay is easy to make the same day as the wedding. But the day before the wedding wash the handkerchief and soak it in liquid starch. Iron the handkerchief once it is dry.

1 standard bunch 20 violets with leaves
pretty handkerchief, 12 inches square
2 yards ¼-inch-wide satin ribbon
plastic sandwich bag
2 facial tissues, folded in half lengthwise
rubber bands

3. Place the violets in the center of the handkerchief and gather the corners up evenly around the stems.

Secure the handkerchief with a rubber band just underneath the violets.

4. From the middle of the ribbon, begin wrapping the handle at the bottom of the stems, neatly criss-crossing the ribbon in front, then in back, then in front again, all the way up the handle. To finish, tie a bow at the top.

3

4

Camille

CAMELLIA: Perfected Loveliness
Unabashed Excellence

Alphonsine du Plessis was a Parisian courtesan in the early nineteenth century famed for her remarkable beauty, her lovers, and her early death. She inspired a novel, an opera, a play, and a classic film starring Greta Garbo. *Camille* dramatized the story of this alluring woman who carried white camellias every day except the five days a month she carried red ones.

Camellias are not easy to work with, but their pristine beauty makes them more than worthwhile. It's wise to have some extra flowers on hand to replace any that bruise. They should be picked as close as possible to the time of the wedding and placed in the refrigerator. Do not mist them.

24 camellia flowers on stems, with leaves
2 yards 6-inch-wide lace
large floral foam bouquet holder with
slanted handle (page 107)
9-inch piece 21-gauge wire

Camellias are very delicate and bruise when barely touched, so work holding only the stems. Do not touch the petals to anything or they will turn brown.

On the day of the wedding, soak the floral foam holder in cool water until no air bubbles appear.

Make a small hook in one end of the wire, then thread the other end of the wire through the edge of the lace, every $^{1}/_{2}$ inch, gathering it into a ruffle.

Attach lace ruffle to holder, securing it to the base with the wire.

Choose perfect flowers. Remove all but the two leaves closest to each flower.

Cut the camellia stems to $2^{1}/_{2}$- to 4 inches and stick them into the floral foam, starting in the center. Cover the foam with flowers, and stick stems into the side of the holder all around to form the outer edge of the bouquet.

Something Blue

FORGET-ME-NOT: Keepsake; Love—Pure and True   Blue is the rarest color of flower. Blue flowers are planted in the garden especially to attract butterflies, bees, and birds. There is a story that in the Garden of Eden, when Adam had nearly finished naming all the animals and plants, one tiny unnoticed blue flower cried, "Forget me not," so he gave her that name. In another famous garden, Lady Chatterley's gamekeeper planted forget-me-nots between her thighs and declared, "There's forget-me-nots in the right place!"

48 forget-me-nots
6 to 8 large ivy leaves (about the size of your hand)
6 yards 1½-inch-wide satin ribbon
a love letter
vinyl tape
dark green florist tape
21-gauge wire
corsage pin

This bouquet will look fresh if it is kept cool, so it can be made the day before the wedding.

The mushy stems of forget-me-nots are vulnerable and must be groomed with care. Carefully, using scissors, remove all but the two leaves closest to each flower. As you work, separate the straight stems from the curved ones and keep the flowers in water.

Starting with the straight-stemmed flowers, form a round bouquet. Tape the stems together. Add the curved stems around the outside edge, taping them in place as you work.

Cut the ribbon into 30-inch pieces. Make three loops in each piece of ribbon and secure it with a 10-inch piece of wire.

Using florist tape, attach one ivy leaf to each ribbon wire just beneath the bow.

Circle the bouquet with the wired bows, ivy leaves on the bottom, and tape them to the stems.

Cut the stems and wires straight across the bottom.

Roll the love letter into a small cylinder and tuck into bouquet.

To finish, wrap the handle with the remaining ribbon and secure it with a corsage pin. Keep in a cool place until the ceremony.

Making the Bouquets

Choose

Begin by choosing the flowers. Use this book as a guide to help you decide which ones you want in the bridal bouquet and the attendants' bouquets, as well as for the boutonnieres. Ask your local nurseryman or florist if the flowers you like will be available in your area at the time you plan to have your wedding. If you can, arrange to visit the nearest wholesale flower mart; it is a wonderful experience, and the prices are low. Usually, however, you will need a resale license from your state to purchase flowers there.

A few weeks before the wedding call your florist and place an order for the flowers you want. Always order a few more flowers than you will need because some stems will have more blooms on them than others, some flowers will be broken or bruised, and you want every bloom you use to be perfect.

It is a very good idea to practice making the bouquets ahead of time. You will be able to see how long the process takes so you will leave plenty of time to make the real bouquets for the big day.

Groom

When you bring your flowers home you must care for them properly to make them last and look their best. Fill your kitchen sink with warm water. Unwrap the flowers and groom them by removing unwanted leaves and thorns according to the "recipe" for the bouquet you are going to create. Gently pull off any unsightly petals. Those that are dry, broken, bruised, or torn should be removed.

Fill a large container with cool water. Put the stems in the sink and cut them with a sharp knife under water on an angle to expose more of the water-absorbing cells inside the stem. Then put the flowers in the container of cool water and store them in a cool place. If you want to force flower buds to open, cut the stems at an angle under water, place them in a container of hot (not boiling) water and set them in a sunny area. To prevent flowers from opening further, put them in water in the refrigerator.

Woody stems, like those of lilac, need to be pounded at the bottom to break the fibers apart. Dip the bottom of each stem into boiling water for 45 seconds, then put into cool water.

Wire and Tape

For some bouquets you will need to wire and tape the flowers. This will support their stems, prevent the flower head from breaking off, and make the stems bendable so you can place them exactly where you wish. Use cloth-covered 24-gauge wire for small and delicate flowers, and heavier 21-gauge wire for roses and most other flowers. You can buy special wires for stephanotis. On one end these wires have a cotton reservoir to soak in water before use. Wire of various weight, as well as stephanotis wires. are available at crafts and florist supply stores.

Use florist tape, also available from crafts or florist supply stores, to bind stems together or to secure flowers to a wire. Where stronger tape is needed, or the tape will be wet, florists use a sticky green vinyl tape.

Wire, tapes and supplies like the floral foam bouquet holder, tulle rounds, fabric glue, bouquet collar, faux pearl and crystal sprays, and corsage and boutonniere pins can also be easily found in crafts and florist supply stores.

Florist tape is used to wrap wired stems and to attach flowers to wire. It sticks to itself, but not to any other surface. It is available in several colors. Vinyl tape (bottom) is used for its strength in securing stems together to form a handle and its resistance to water. Sticks for a hot glue gun are used to attach beads or jewels.

Basic tools for working with flowers and constructing bouquets include (top, left to right): snippers, used to cut greens and vines; branch cutters, for branches and thick or woody stems; a florist's knife to cut flower stems so their water-absorbing cells are not crushed. (center, left to right): hot glue gun; rose stripper to remove leaves and thorns from rose stems; wire cutter. (bottom left to right): spray mist bottle; ribbon scissors; clippers for trimming stem handles.

1. The delicate stem of the dahlia must be reinforced with a wire to hold its heavy head. Simply poke the wire into the thick green calyx just under the petals, then wind the wire around the stem only once and tape.

2. The pincushion flower or a chrysanthemum can be reinforced by poking a wire through the flower from underneath. Bend the top inch of wire like a hairpin, and pull it back into the center of the flower and tape.

3. To create a four-loop bow, fold the ribbon in half, then in half again. Fold a wire around the center of the loops and twist it.

4. The rose is wired by piercing the calyx, or hip, with the wire. Fold the wire parallel to the stem.

5 6 7 8

5.   Wind the long end of the wire around the stem several times.

6.   Starting underneath the flower head, wind the florist tape around the wired stem. Pull the tape at an angle, stretching it as you work.

7.   Wind the tape tightly, covering the wired stem.

8.   For some bouquets you will need to cut off all but 2 inches of the stem. Then wire the flower through the green calyx and tape the wire as if it were the stem.

Method

Some bouquets should be made in your hand. Simply hold the flowers loosely by their stems and move them around so they show their faces and form the shape you want. Then secure them in place with tape. You can make some bouquets in a container, then tape the stems together after you lift the flowers out.

Bouquets that cascade or are designed to be held in the crook of your arm are most easily constructed on a flat surface. Lay the flowers on a table in an outline of the desired shape, stems pointing in the same direction to create a handle (page 15). Starting opposite the handle, layer the rest of the flowers so they cover the stems of the ones next to them, and fill in the shape. Tape the stems together every time you add five flowers.

To construct some bouquets you will first need to make several clusters. Layer the materials, largest on the bottom, smallest on top, and tape the stems together. Tape the cluster to a wire and cover the wire with tape. A boutonniere is a cluster finished off with a bit of ribbon and a pearl-tipped pin. To finish your bouquet, decorate the handle with beautiful ribbon and add a bow and streamers that complements the flowers and the dress.

To make a round bouquet with flowers like roses and dahlias that have rigid stems, place them one at a time in a container with a wide opening. Lean the flowers against one edge of the container with the bottom of the stem resting against the opposite side. The stems will cross each other. Pick them up with both hands and tape the stems together where they cross.

Another way to make a circular-shaped bouquet is to place a row of flowers around the edge of a container with the heads hanging on the rim. Gently hold the flowers in both hands, picking them up below the heads. Adjust their position if necessary and tape the stems together to form the handle.

1. *First cover the bottom of the trimmed stems with one end of the ribbon and secure it with a rubber band one inch from the bottom.*

2. *Then holding the ribbon at a slight angle wind it tightly, covering the rubber band and the stems.*

3. *Finally, fold the end of the ribbon under to hide the raw edge, and secure it to the handle with a corsage pin.*

Care

To care for the bouquet until the wedding follow the instructions in the "recipe." Flowers require a lot of water to stay fresh. They absorb water through their petals and stems. Most should be misted using a spray bottle of clean water and put in a cool place or in the refrigerator. Heavy misting can cause water spots on some flower petals, but hydrangeas will drink all the water you can spray on them.

Some of the bouquets should be covered loosely with a large plastic bag to avoid drying out. Your refrigerator's humidity is lower than the humidity in commercial refrigerators and the plastic covering will help the flowers retain their moisture. When it is time for the first photographs to be taken, dry the stems thoroughly and shake off any excess water so no drops get on the wedding gown.

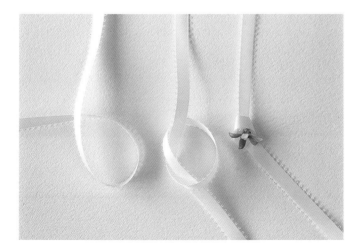

To make a lovers' knot, cross one end of a ribbon behind itself, making a loop. Thread the ribbon over and through the loop. Pull the ribbon into a loose knot. Tuck a small flower into the knot, if desired, and draw the ribbon tight enough to hold the flower.

Acknowledgments

Like flowers in the Victorian flower language, the names of those who helped me make this book have taken on significant and special meanings. I am so grateful for the participation of each one of them in helping me to realize this dream. I thank them with all my heart for the qualities of each, and their contributions to *Bouquets*.

⁓

Richard—perfection, brilliance, kind spirit

Susy—"The flowers will speak to you"

Maggie—loyalty, love, presence

Miki—excitement, inspiration

Matt and James—faith, total support–tech and personal

Karen and Mandy—taste and generosity

Claudia—time, effort, and artist's eyes

Sunshine—guidance and confidence

Lena—acceptance and encouragement

Marilyn—discernment and constancy

Mom—belief and sharing treasures

Lisa—clarity and purity

Ivy—cheer and work

Laurie and Kennah, Jasmin and Angela—feminine graces

Michelle—welcoming

Amy—vision

Wendy—pride

Suki—learning

Linda—shelter

Pat—perfect connection

Dimitri and Michele—contribution

and Floyd is everything—faith, support, generosity, care and love—in so many ways for 35 years

⁓

Karen Metz, owner of Marina Morrison Ltd. Bridal Salon in San Francisco, provided all of the exquisite designer wedding gowns in *Bouquets*. I am ever grateful for her generous contribution and for the direction of her brilliant manager, Mandy Wong.

Thank you to Leslie Stoker, Julie Ho, Michael Gray, Caroline Enright-Lederer, the team at Stewart, Tabori & Chang, and to Linda Sunshine who nurtured me and *Bouquets* so kindly through this year.

Designed by Lisa Vaughn for Two of Cups Studio
The text of this book was composed in Adobe Garamond, Amphora, and Poetica
Printed and bound in Singapore by Tien Wah Press